SNAKES

KING COBRAS

James E. Gerholdt
ABDO & Daughters

Published by Abdo & Daughters, 4940 Viking Drive, Suite 622, Edina, Minnesota 55435.

Library bound edition distributed by Rockbottom Books, Pentagon Tower, P.O. Box 36036, Minneapolis, Minnesota 55435.

Printed in the United States.

Cover Photo credit: Photo Researchers, Inc.
Interior Photo credits: Photo Researchers, Inc. pages 5, 9, 15
Animals Animals, pages 11, 17, 19
Paul Freed, pages 7, 21

Edited by Julie Berg

Gerholdt, James E., 1943
     King Cobras / James E. Gerholdt.
          p. cm. — (Snakes)
Includes bibliographical references (p. 23) and index.
Summary: Describes personal characteristics, habitat, food habits, and defense mechanisms of this reptile whose bite can kill a human and even an elephant.
ISBN 1-56239-516-5
1. King Cobra—Juvenile literature. [1. King Cobra. 2. Cobras. 3. Poisonous snakes 4. Snakes] I. Title. II. Series: Gerholdt, James E.,   1943- Snakes.
QL666.064G47   1995
597.96—dc20   95-4730
                                                           CIP
                                                            AC

About the Author
Jim Gerholdt has been studying reptiles and amphibians for more than 40 years. He has presented lectures and displays throughout the state of Minnesota for 9 years. He is a founding member of the Minnesota Herpetological Society and is active in conservation issues involving reptiles and amphibians in India and Aruba, as well as Minnesota.

Contents

KING COBRAS

King cobras belong to one of the 11 snake families. A snake is a **reptile**, which is a **vertebrate**. This means they have a backbone, just like a human.

Cobras are **cold blooded.** They get their body temperature from lying in the sun, on a warm log, or the warm ground. If they are too cool, their bodies won't work. If they get too hot, they will die. This is because their bodies need to be at a certain temperature. These snakes are called king cobras because they eat other snakes.

The king cobra likes to lie in the sun and warm itself on a rock.

SIZES

The king cobra is the largest **venomous** snake in the world. It is very slender. The length of a snake is measured from the tip of the nose to the tip of the tail. The longest king cobra ever found was over 18 feet (5.5 m)! The average size of an adult is 10 to 13 feet (3 to 4 m).

A large king cobra is a very awesome sight. It can stand as high as four feet (1.2 m) when it raises the front part of the body off the ground and expands its **hood.**

The cobra is known for its hood.

hood

King cobras are very slender and long.

COLORS

King cobras are not brightly colored. They are usually brown or olive green, or even yellowish. Some of them have light crossbands on the front of the body. Their bellies are a lighter color, usually a pale yellow. The rear of the body and the tail are black.

Baby king cobras are more brightly colored than the adults. They are banded with black and white markings. The colors and markings vary with the different areas in which they are found.

Some king cobras have light crossbands on the front of their body.

WHERE THEY LIVE

King cobras are found in more than one kind of **habitat**. They like open areas, such as grassland or a **cultivated** field.

The king cobra is a good swimmer. It likes water, and is often found near streams.

King cobras are also found in forests, **bamboo thickets**, and cluttered **mangrove swamps**. In zoos, they will spend time on branches and logs above the cage floor.

King cobras live in many types of habitats.

WHERE THEY ARE FOUND

King cobras are found in many different Asian countries. But they are not very common in any one place.

Most of the king cobras seen in North American zoos come from Thailand. They are also found in India, southern China, Vietnam, the Philippines, Hong Kong, Cambodia, Malaya, and some Indonesian islands.

China

India

Hong Kong

Thailand

Vietnam

Malaya

Cambodia

Philippines

Indonesia

*King cobras
are found in
Southeast Asia,
China and India.*

Detail
Area

SENSES

King cobras and humans share four of the same senses. They have very poor eyesight, and have trouble seeing anything that isn't moving. But their eyesight is better than most snakes. They have round **pupils** because they are active during the daylight hours.

Like all snakes, king cobras cannot hear. But they can feel **vibrations** through bones in the lower jaw.

The snake's most important sense organ is its tongue, with which it smells. Without the tongue, a king cobra could not find its food. Many experts think the king cobra is the smartest of all the snakes.

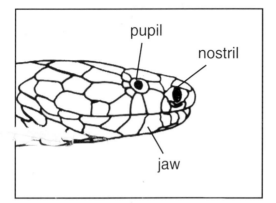

pupil

nostril

jaw

King cobras have very poor eyesight and have trouble seeing anything that isn't moving.

DEFENSE

The king cobra's colors help it blend with its surroundings. This is called **camouflage**. It is the most important defense against its enemies. Because it is so big and so **venomous**, a king cobra has few enemies, except humans.

If a king cobra is threatened, it will raise the front part of the body off of the ground and spread a narrow **hood**. It will also hiss loudly. If this doesn't work, it will strike and bite. The bite is very **poisonous**, and can kill a human. Even elephants have died from the bite of a king cobra.

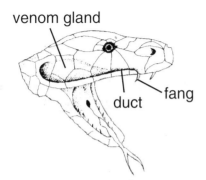

venom gland

duct

fang

Venom is made in the venom glands. The glands are on both sides of the snake's head and lie outside the main jaw muscles toward the back of the head. When the snake bites, the venom travels from each gland through the ducts and the hollow fangs, and into the prey.

If a king cobra is threatened, it will raise the front part of its body into a defensive position and spread its hood.

FOOD

King cobras eat other snakes, including **venomous** ones like the smaller common cobras. King cobras are active hunters. They spend much of their time seeking food.

When a snake is spotted by the king cobra, it is chased and caught. The king cobra's venom kills its prey quickly. Then the prey is swallowed, usually head first.

Sometimes the king cobra loses the battle. A **reticulated** python once killed the cobra that attacked it, using its powerful **constriction**. King cobras also eat lizards and frogs.

A king cobra eating another snake.

BABIES

Baby king cobras hatch from eggs. The mother lays 20 to 50 eggs. The larger the mother, the more eggs she will lay.

The king cobra is the world's only snake that builds a nest. The female will scrape together dirt and leaves, using loops of her body.

Sometimes the nest has two parts: the lower one for the eggs, and the upper one for the female. While the eggs are **incubating**, both the male and the female will guard the nest.

When the babies hatch, they are about 18 inches (46 cm) long. They shed their skin for the first time at the age of seven to ten days. This is called **ecdysis.** It takes place whenever the old skin gets too small for the snake.

A newly hatched king cobra.

GLOSSARY

Bamboo Thickets - Bamboo that grows close together. Bamboo is a woody treelike grass with a very tall, stiff, hollow stem that has hard, thick joints.

Camouflage (CAM-a-flaj) - The ability to blend in with the surroundings.

Cold-blooded - Animals that get their body temperature from an outside source.

Constriction (kun-STRICK-shun) - To squeeze or compress together.

Cultivate (KULL-tih-vait) - To loosen the ground around growing plants to kill weeds.

Duct - A tube in the body for carrying liquid or air.

Ecdysis (ek-DIE-sis) - The process of shedding the old skin.

Gland - An organ in the body which makes and gives out some substance.

Habitat (HAB-uh-tat) - The type of environment in which an animal lives.

Hood - An expansion of a snake's head.

Incubate (INK-u-bate) - To sit on eggs to hatch them.

Mangrove swamp - Tropical trees or shrubs with a dense root system that grows in coastal areas.

Poison (POY-zun) - Any substance that is very dangerous to life or health when it is breathed or swallowed.

Pupil (PEW-pill) - The opening in the eye's center where light enters.

Reptile (REP-tile) - A scaly-skinned animal with a backbone.

Reticulated (ruh-TICK-u-lay-ted) - Having lines across the body that look like a net.

Venom (VEN-um) - Poison that is used to kill animals for food.

Vertebrate (VER-tah-brit) - An animal with a backbone.

Vibration (vie-BRAY-shun) - A quivering or trembling motion.

BIBLIOGRAPHY

Coborn, John. *The Atlas of Snakes of the World.* T.F.H. Publications, Inc., 1991.

Keng, Francis Lim Leong and Monty Lee Tat-Mong. *Fascinating Snakes of Southeast Asia - An Introduction.* Tropical Press, 1989.

Mehrtens, John M. *Living Snakes of the World in Color.* Sterling Publishing Company, 1987.

Phelps, Tony. *Poisonous Snakes,* -Revised Edition. Blandford Press, 1989.

Index